RECEIVE YOUR HEALING:

WHAT YOU SAY JESUS WILL DO

GLORIA COPELAND

JESUS IS LORD®

KENNETH COPELAND PUBLICATIONS

I0811525

Unless otherwise noted, all scripture is from the *New King James Version* of the Bible, © 1982 by Thomas Nelson Inc.

Scripture quotations marked *New International Version* are from *The Holy Bible, New International Version* © 1973, 1978, 1984, 2011 by Biblica Inc. Used by permission. All rights reserved worldwide.

Scripture quotations marked *Amplified Bible, Classic Edition* are from the *Amplified® Bible,* © 1954, 1958, 1962, 1964, 1965, 1987 by The Lockman Foundation. Used by permission.

Scripture quotations marked *English Standard Version* are from *The Holy Bible, English Standard Version®* Text Edition: 2016, © 2001 by Crossway, a publishing ministry of Good News Publishers. Used by permission. All rights reserved.

Scripture quotations marked *The Message* are from *The Message* © 1993, 1994, 1995, 1996, 2000, 2001, 2002. Used by permission of Nav-Press Publishing Group.

Scripture quotations marked *New Living Translation* are from the *Holy Bible, New Living Translation* © 1996, 2004, 2007 by Tyndale Charitable Trust. Used by permission of Tyndale House Publishers.

Scripture quotations marked *King James Version* are from the *King James Version* of the Bible.

Receive Your Healing: What You Say, Jesus Will Do

ISBN 978-1-60463-571-3 30-0591
30 29 28 27 26 25 6 5 4 3 2 1

©2025 Gloria Copeland

Kenneth Copeland Publications
Fort Worth, TX 76192-0001

For more information about Kenneth Copeland Ministries, visit kcm.org or call 1-800-600-7395 (U.S. only) or +1-817-852-6000.

Printed in the United States of America. All rights reserved under International Copyright Law. No part of this book may be reproduced or transmitted in any form or by any means, electronic or mechanical, including photocopying, recording, or by any information storage and retrieval system, without the written permission of the publisher.

TABLE OF CONTENTS

PREFACE

Years ago, the Lord gave me a message to preach at Healing School that turned out to be what you might call a spiritual game changer. Simple and straight from the Word, in one sense it wasn't anything new. Yet the results it produced in our healing services were nothing short of amazing.

In the first six months I preached it, more people got their healing than ever before. More miracles happened in the services. More blind eyes were opened than I'd seen in twenty years of ministry.

One blind man who got his sight was ninety years old! He'd been specifically led of the Lord to attend Healing School that year, and he'd come with a great sense of expectancy. After listening intently to the message, he came forward for prayer. On the way back to his seat, he began to see!

In another meeting, a woman showed up who, in addition to being blind, had a burning desire to go into ministry. She heard me preach the same message, came forward to have hands laid on her and was healed. She went away shouting, "Hallelujah! I'm going to work for the Lord!"

What message was it that enabled people to lay hold of such miracles? Simply this: *Jesus is Anointed to heal, and He's easy to receive from!*

That's a very basic message, but it's one we all need to hear over and over again. Every time I preach it, it strengthens my faith. It counters the lie the devil continually peddles that sometimes getting healed is hard. It reminds me that Jesus' Anointing is still as strong as ever, and that He can heal me of anything, anytime, anywhere, just as easily as He healed people in the Gospels, where multitudes "sought to touch Him, for power went out from Him and healed them all" (Luke 6:19).

"But Gloria," someone might say, "things are different these days than they were in the Gospels. Back then, Jesus was here on earth ministering to people personally. Now He's ascended back to heaven."

I know. But His Ascension didn't change who He is and what He does. Acts 1:11 makes that clear. It says, "This same Jesus, who has been taken from you into heaven, will come back in the same way..." *(New International Version).*

This same Jesus! Those are the words the Lord quickened to me all those years ago when He first gave me this message—and they are good news! They assure us that the Jesus we see in the Gospels is the same Jesus who's coming back for the Church, which means He is the same Jesus today.

He hasn't changed one bit. If it was easy for people to receive healing from Him when He was on earth in a natural body, it's easy for us to receive healing from Him now. He is "the same yesterday, today, and forever" (Hebrews 13:8).

CHAPTER 1

WHO IS JESUS?

CHAPTER 1

WHO IS JESUS?

One of the most wonderful things about Jesus has always been how willing He is to heal people. When He was on earth, He never turned away anyone who came to Him for healing…and they came to Him by the thousands.

They came to Him no matter how sick or seemingly beyond help they were. They came to Him even though they had experienced rejection from others and felt shame because of their condition. People suffering from every kind of infirmity imaginable flocked to Jesus, because they saw His compassion.

There was an approachability about Him. Those who weren't normally welcome at religious gatherings, like the blind and the lame, for instance, "came to Him in the temple, and He healed them" (Matthew 21:14). Even the chief priests and scribes noticed "the wonderful things that He did" (verse 15). And though they often criticized Him for doing those things, they couldn't get Him to stop.

Regardless of their opposition, Jesus went right on doing the work God had sent and Anointed Him to do.

He went on carrying out His mission.

One of the first places He publicly announced that mission was in His hometown of Nazareth. As Luke 4 says:

> He came to Nazareth, where He had been brought up. And as His custom was, He went into the synagogue on the Sabbath day, and stood up to read. And He was handed the book of the prophet Isaiah. And when He had opened the book, He found the place where it was written: "The Spirit of the LORD is upon Me, because He has anointed Me to preach the gospel to the poor; He has sent Me to heal the brokenhearted, to proclaim liberty to the captives and recovery of sight to the blind, to set at liberty those who are oppressed; to proclaim the acceptable year of the LORD." Then He closed the book, and gave it back to the attendant and sat down. And the eyes of all who were in the synagogue were fixed on Him. And He began to say to them, "Today this Scripture is fulfilled in your hearing." So all bore witness to Him, and marveled at the gracious words which proceeded out of His mouth… (verses 16-22).

Notice Jesus really got people's attention there. They fixed their eyes on Him because, while they were familiar with the passage of Scripture He read from Isaiah 61, it sounded different when Jesus read it. He spoke with

Anointing and authority. He made the statement powerfully and prophetically.

Have you ever been around a person who spoke anointed words? Their words seemed to hang in the air, ready to produce supernatural results for those who would receive them. That's how it seemed to the people in the synagogue that day. They marveled at Jesus' "gracious words."

The word *gracious* means "disposed to show favors." It perfectly describes not only how Jesus sounded, but also what He was proclaiming about Himself and His ministry. He said He came to proclaim, as the *Amplified Bible, Classic Edition* puts it, "the day when the salvation and free favors of God profusely abound" (verse 19).

Have you been to a wedding where the host passed out free favors? I have, and when those free gifts are handed out, everyone smiles and rejoices. Throughout Jesus' earthly ministry, that's how people who believed what Jesus said responded to Him. They ran to Him and shouted His praises because He preached a message of hope, encouragement and power. He preached that it was time for the free favors of God to profusely abound.

If you've ever wondered why Jesus is so good, it's because the Father is so good. You can see how good God is by watching Jesus, because He is the visible representation of God the Father. "He who has seen Me has seen the Father," Jesus said (John 14:9). And Psalm 145:8-9 says the Father "is gracious and full of compassion, slow to anger and great in mercy. The LORD is good to all, and His tender mercies are over all His works."

You don't have to twist God's arm into showering you with favors. All you have to do is believe what Jesus said about it, come to Him, and receive!

CHAPTER 2

JESUS IN ACTION

CHAPTER 2

JESUS IN ACTION

When Jesus was on earth ministering in the synagogues and the Temple, as we have seen, people quickly realized that His gracious words also carried divine power. Everywhere He went, those who heard Him "were astonished at His teaching, for He taught them as one having authority, and not as the scribes" (Mark 1:22).

Even the devil recognized the authority of Jesus' words. They hit him with such power, he was left shaking in his boots. The Word Jesus preached was so strong, the devil thought he was about to be destroyed.

In one instance, an unclean spirit that was in a man in the synagogue cried out saying, "'Let us alone! What have we to do with You, Jesus of Nazareth? Did you come to destroy us? I know who You are—the Holy One of God!'

"But Jesus rebuked him, saying, 'Be quiet, and come out of him!' And when the unclean spirit had convulsed him and cried out with a loud voice, he came out of him" (verses 24-26). That demon spirit had held that man captive, and Jesus came to set the captives free. So, that's what He did.

The people in the synagogue who saw it happen "were all amazed, so that they questioned among themselves, saying, 'What is this? What new doctrine is this? For with authority He commands even the unclean spirits, and they obey Him'" (verse 27).

In addition to teaching in the synagogue, Jesus also ministered to people in their homes. When he went to Peter's house, for example, and found his mother-in-law sick with a fever, without hesitation Jesus "took her by the hand and lifted her up, and immediately the fever left her" (Mark 1:31).

She didn't even have to ask Jesus to pray for her! He ministered goodness, kindness and mercy to her because He always went about doing good. In fact, that's how Peter later summed up Jesus' ministry. He said, "God anointed Jesus of Nazareth with the Holy Spirit and with power, who went about doing good and healing all who were oppressed by the devil, for God was with Him" (Acts 10:38).

Wherever He went, Jesus ministered healing and deliverance to people. So everywhere He went, crowds of people showed up. They even showed up at Peter's house that day. When those in the community heard Jesus was there, "they brought to Him all who were sick and those who were demon-possessed. And the whole city was gathered together at the door" (Mark 1:32-33).

The whole city! That is a large number of people!

Think about that. This wasn't a crowd of healthy, vibrant people looking for Jesus. These people were struggling with sickness, disease and demon possession.

If you've ever been around large numbers of hurting people, it can feel overwhelming or even oppressive. But instead of being burdened down by the magnitude of the need, Jesus sprang into action. Doing what He was Anointed to do, He spoke with authority the words of the Father, and did the Father's works by ministering life to the people. "He healed many who were sick with various diseases, and cast out many demons..." (verse 34).

Ministering to such a massive crowd must have been exhausting. And yet, do you know what Jesus did afterward? He got up the next morning a long time before daylight, "went out and departed to a solitary place; and there He prayed" (verse 35).

Jesus stayed ready to minister God's power to people! No matter how demanding His day or how physically weary He might have been, He spent time in prayer. He pulled aside to fellowship with His heavenly Father.

Because Jesus *was* in constant communion with God, He was always able to say what He heard the Father say. Because Jesus stayed in continual contact with His Father, He could do the Father's works and minister to people God's lovingkindness. (This is also how we, as believers, are to operate in the kingdom of God.)

When Jesus' disciples found Him praying the morning after His massive healing meeting, they said, "Everyone is looking for You" (verse 37). They thought He should keep ministering in the same place because He'd been so well-received there. But Jesus had already found the will of the Father in prayer. So His response was, "Let us go into the next towns, that I may preach there also, because for this purpose I have come forth" (verse 38).

What was Jesus preaching? "The Spirit of the Lord [is] upon Me, because He has anointed Me [the Anointed One, the Messiah] to preach the good news (the Gospel) to the poor; He has sent Me to announce release to the captives and recovery of sight to the blind, to send forth as delivered those who are oppressed [who are downtrodden, bruised, crushed, and broken down by calamity], to proclaim the accepted and acceptable year of the Lord [the day when salvation and the free favors of God profusely abound]" (Luke 4:18-19, *Amplified Bibe, Classic Edition).*

What was His purpose? "How God anointed Jesus of Nazareth with the Holy Ghost and with power: who went about doing good, and healing all that were oppressed of the devil; for God was with him" (Acts 10:38, *King James Version).*

CHAPTER 3

JESUS' MINISTRY TODAY

CHAPTER 3

JESUS' MINISTRY TODAY

Jesus is doing the same things today that we read about in the Gospels! He is still the same Jesus who walked the earth with Peter and the other disciples, and He is still giving life to whomever will receive Him.

In fact, if you've been born again, you actually have His life inside you because you have His Holy Spirit within you. That means you can receive healing anytime you need it. For as Romans 8:11 says, "If the Spirit of Him who raised Jesus from the dead dwells in you, He who raised Christ from the dead will also give life to your mortal bodies through His Spirit who dwells in you."

In other words, the same Spirit who raised Jesus from the dead is the same Spirit who heals your body today!

Think about that: Jesus is the Healer. What is it that you need Him to do for you right now? What do you need in your body? Is there a sickness or disease you have experienced for so long that you have gotten used to it? Is there something that you think is too hard for God to do? If so, let all your limitations go.

God has body parts, and He will give them to you! He can replace a kidney or a liver. He can make organs live again. He can give you a new heart, a new eye, a new eardrum, or anything else you might need. There is nothing too hard for God. He's not like a human doctor; He is God Almighty, and He has resurrection power!

I remember one woman who came to Healing School who didn't have a chin. While hearing the Word preached, she began expecting God to give her one. She had never really thought about believing for that before, but while the Word was going forth, faith rose up inside her.

Looking around at the other people in the meeting, she thought, *What kind of chin do I want?* She picked out one that suited her and believed for one just like it. Satisfied in her heart that she had received, soon afterward she began to feel a tingle in the area where her chin should be. Sure enough, she received a fully formed chin! That is the working of miracles!

In another instance, a little boy who had been born without nostrils came to Healing School with his mother. The doctors had said he would have to wait until he turned twelve years old, when his bones would be fully formed, before he could have the operation that would correct the problem. I noticed during the service that the boy was sniffing in an unusual way, and found out that while hearing the Word, he had received holes in his nose! No one laid hands on him. He received by hearing and believing the Word of God.

Exactly what was he hearing from the Word?

He was hearing about how Jesus healed people in the Bible. When I'm teaching Healing School, I especially love reading the scriptural accounts of Jesus' healings. He never told anyone, as religious tradition sometimes teaches today, that it might not be God's will to heal them. He never complicated matters by suggesting they might have to stay sick awhile longer for reasons they might not understand.

On the contrary, Jesus always made it the easiest thing in the world for people to receive healing from Him, and I am going to prove that to you in this book. By taking you through the scriptures that describe how Jesus healed people back when He was on earth, I am going to show you how easy it is for *you* to receive from Him today.

CHAPTER 4

EXAMPLES OF JESUS HEALING PEOPLE

EXAMPLES OF JESUS HEALING PEOPLE:

THE LEPER

"If You are willing, You can make me clean."

> Now a leper came to Him, imploring Him, kneeling down to Him and saying to Him, "If You are willing, You can make me clean." Then Jesus, moved with compassion, stretched out His hand and touched him, and said to him, "I am willing; be cleansed." As soon as He had spoken, immediately the leprosy left him, and he was cleansed. And He strictly warned him and sent him away at once, and said to him, "See that you say nothing to anyone; but go your way, show yourself to the priest, and offer for your cleansing those things which Moses commanded, as a testimony to them" (Mark 1:40-44).

To understand the significance of this healing, it's important to know how lepers were treated during biblical times. They were viewed as unclean and treated as outcasts. No one came near them. Considered the lowest in society, they were forced to live as beggars. Some people even viewed leprosy as a divine punishment for a person's sins. So, lepers experienced a lot of rejection.

When someone is continually rejected, they can become hard-hearted and angry, or even feel like giving up completely. But the leper we read about in Mark 1, though he might have been struggling with such feelings, came to Jesus anyway. In Luke's account, it says he "fell on his face and implored Him" (Luke 5:12). He humbled himself before Jesus and begged for His help.

Like many people today, this man was confident that Jesus *could* heal him, but he was unsure if He *would*. So, he made this simple statement, "If You are willing, You can make me clean."

How did Jesus respond?

He did not turn away, as others surely would have. Instead, He moved toward the man with compassion. That's how Jesus always responded when someone came to Him for healing or deliverance. He never ignored or rejected those who approached Him asking for help. He always provided what they needed.

This man needed to know that Jesus was *willing* to cleanse him of leprosy. So, to activate the man's faith, Jesus not only said what the leper needed to hear, He reached out to touch this man who had been deemed untouchable by society. "I am willing," He said, "be cleansed."

The leper believed it and received his healing!

This is a wonderful example of Jesus' willingness. So,

let it encourage you. If you've been told that sometimes Jesus is unwilling to heal, and that has kept you from receiving the healing He provided for you, right now, you can put that sense of uncertainty behind you forever. You can believe and receive your healing because Jesus is saying to you now the same words He said to the leper in this passage of Scripture: "I am willing; be healed."

In each biblical account of healing, whatever people said to Jesus, He did. He was so pliable, so easy. Jesus wanted to accommodate people. He came to set the captives free and bring deliverance. Anyone who would believe His words could receive from Him.

EXAMPLES OF JESUS HEALING PEOPLE:

THE PARALYTIC MAN

"When He saw their faith, He said to him, 'Man, your sins are forgiven you.... Rise up and walk.'"

Now it happened on a certain day, as He was teaching, that there were Pharisees and teachers of the law sitting by, who had come out of every town of Galilee, Judea, and Jerusalem. And the power of the Lord was present to heal them. Then behold, men brought on a bed a man who was paralyzed, whom they sought to bring in and lay before Him. And when they could not find how they might bring him in, because of the crowd, they went up on the housetop and let him down with his bed through the tiling into the midst before Jesus. When He saw their faith, He said to him, "Man, your sins are forgiven you." And the scribes and the Pharisees began to reason, saying, "Who is this who speaks blasphemies? Who can forgive sins but God alone?" But when Jesus perceived their thoughts, He answered and said to them, "Why are you reasoning in your hearts? Which is easier, to say, 'Your sins are forgiven you,' or to say, 'Rise up and walk'? But that you may know that the Son of Man has power on

> earth to forgive sins"—He said to the man who was paralyzed, "I say to you, arise, take up your bed, and go to your house" (Luke 5:17-24).

We see this over and over again in the Gospels: People received from Jesus by simply believing His Word, not by reasoning and trying to be an expert. The Pharisees and teachers of the law found this out for themselves the day Jesus healed the paralytic. The power of the Lord was present to heal them even before the paralytic man arrived, yet not one scribe or Pharisee was healed.

Why didn't they receive? They were not in a position to receive. They were trying to be experts. Rather than honoring Jesus and simply believing His words, they were critical and faultfinding. They were there to try to catch Him saying something wrong.

Don't ever have a critical attitude toward those who preach the Word. That will make it difficult for you to receive from Jesus. If you can't agree with a particular preacher or ministry, don't criticize them and tear them down. Just leave them alone; find someone else who is preaching the uncompromised Word of God, and believe the Word.

Put yourself in a position to receive by following the example of the paralytic man and his four friends. They came to Jesus in simple faith, determined to get for him the healing he needed. They were so determined to receive from Jesus that when they found they couldn't get into the meeting because there were too many people, they did something dramatic!

They didn't just leave or wait around outside hoping Jesus would come near to them. With their crippled friend on a cot, the four friends climbed onto the top of the house, took off a section of the roof, and lowered the paralyzed man down on his bed in front of Jesus.

That's the kind of thing faith friends will do! They will stand with you and believe God with you in the face of discouraging circumstances. Of course, in this instance, it wasn't just the friends who had faith. The man they were carrying must have had some too. Otherwise, he wouldn't have agreed to their plan.

Think about that: If you were sick in bed and unable to walk, you would have to agree for someone to take you out of your house. Then if you were unable to get into the place where Jesus was, you would have to agree to be carried onto the rooftop on your bed and be let down through the ceiling. If you didn't have a certain amount of faith, you'd say, "I don't think that's a good idea."

So, obviously, all five of these friends had faith—and Jesus saw it! He saw it through their actions. He saw it in their determination to reach Him and in the unusual way they went about getting the paralyzed man into the house.

Faith requires action. When people come to our

meetings and testify to a healing that has taken place in their bodies, many say, "I believed that if I could just get to your meeting and hear the Word of God, I would be healed." Other times, people have said, "I believe that when I return to the doctor, that infirmity will no longer be there."

There are many ways to put action to your faith, and Jesus responded to the actions of the four men who literally dropped their friend into His meeting that day by saying to the one who was paralyzed, "Man, your sins are forgiven you" (Luke 5:20).

Why didn't Jesus say, "You're healed"? Because He always met people where they were. He always said what the Father said, and the Father knows if something is holding someone back from receiving healing. He knows the lies the enemy feeds people that cause them to stay sick.

Apparently, the paralytic man was struggling with one of the enemy's lies. Maybe he thought his sins were too big, and that was hindering his ability to receive from God. By telling him, "Your sins are forgiven you," Jesus freed him from that hindrance so he could be healed.

When the scribes and Pharisees heard Jesus tell the man that his sins were forgiven, they became indignant. They reasoned among themselves whether, in their "expert" opinion, Jesus had the ability to forgive sins. Clinging to the critical attitude that had kept them from receiving themselves, they even accused Him of blasphemy.

The paralytic man, however, just took Jesus at His Word. So, when Jesus said to him, "Arise, take up your bed, and go to your house" (Luke 5:24), he did it. He believed he was healed and, acting on Jesus' words, to everyone's amazement, the man got up, picked up his bed and headed home, walking on his own two feet!

Do you see what happened there? That man came to Jesus expecting to be healed, and Jesus responded accordingly. He spoke to the man the words he needed to hear in order to receive what he expected. As a result, not only did the man do what Jesus said, so did the crippling disease that had caused the paralysis. It left the man's body, and he left the meeting that day healed!

EXAMPLES OF JESUS HEALING PEOPLE:

THE BOY WITH A DEVIL

"If You can do anything,

have compassion on us and help us."

And when He [Jesus] came to the disciples, He saw a great multitude around them, and scribes disputing with them. Immediately, when they saw Him, all the people were greatly amazed, and running to Him, greeted Him. And He asked the scribes, "What are you discussing with them?" Then one of the crowd answered and said, "Teacher, I brought You my son, who has a mute spirit. And wherever it seizes him, it throws him down; he foams at the mouth, gnashes his teeth, and becomes rigid. So I spoke to Your disciples, that they should cast it out, but they could not." He answered him and said, "O faithless generation, how long shall I be with you? How long shall I bear with you? Bring him to Me." Then they brought him to Him. And when he saw Him, immediately the spirit convulsed him, and he fell on the ground and wallowed, foaming at the mouth. So He asked his father, "How long has this been happening to him?" And he said, "From childhood. And often he has thrown him both into the

> fire and into the water to destroy him. But if You can do anything, have compassion on us and help us." Jesus said to him, "If you can believe, all things are possible to him who believes." Immediately the father of the child cried out and said with tears, "Lord, I believe; help my unbelief!" When Jesus saw that the people came running together, He rebuked the unclean spirit, saying to it, "Deaf and dumb spirit, I command you, come out of him and enter him no more!" Then the spirit cried out, convulsed him greatly, and came out of him. And he became as one dead, so that many said, "He is dead." But Jesus took him by the hand and lifted him up, and he arose (Mark 9:14-27).

Have you ever asked for prayer, hoping to be healed, and been disappointed? Have you ever gone to a doctor or called ministry prayer lines for healing and seen no results? Were you left wondering, *Can anyone help me?*

If so, let this account of healing in Mark 9 remind you: The answer to that question is *yes!*

It doesn't matter how many times others have prayed for you. It doesn't matter how many well-meaning people have tried unsuccessfully to help you. Jesus still stands before you ready, willing and able to heal you.

There's no sickness too stubborn, no devilish disease too big for Him to handle. He said so to the father of this boy, and that situation looked impossible. Not only was the boy unable to talk; the demon spirit that was plaguing him constantly threw him around. The father said, "Wherever it lays hold of him [so as to make him its own], it dashes him down and convulses him, and he foams [at the mouth] and grinds his teeth, and he [falls into a motionless stupor and] is wasting away" (Mark 9:18, *Amplified Bible, Classic Edition).*

Imagine how desperate this boy's father must have felt!

He was watching his son deteriorate daily. He had already been disappointed by the failure of Jesus' disciples to minister deliverance to the boy, and he wanted no more delays. So, coming to Jesus, he begged Him to do whatever He could to help them.

How did Jesus respond?

He quickly said, "Bring him to Me."

Jesus did not hesitate to take care of this situation, and this same Jesus doesn't hesitate in your life. You can come to Him anytime, anywhere, and He'll be there for you.

He'll even be there for you when you're struggling with doubt. You can see that too, in how He responded to this boy's father. The father wasn't even certain that Jesus could do for his son what was needed. But having heard that Jesus was loving and merciful, and that people were being helped by Him, he presented to Jesus this simple, honest request: "If You can do anything, have compassion on us and help us."

Jesus was looking for faith from this man. For the father to receive his son's healing, Jesus knew the man had to get in agreement with Him. So He answered the father's request with an emphatic faith-building declaration. He said, "All things are possible to him who believes!"

"Lord, I believe;" the father cried, "help my unbelief!"

Notice that although he was ready and willing to believe Jesus' words, at the same time, he was honest in saying that he was still struggling with some unbelief. Also notice how Jesus responded. He didn't chastise him. He did what the man said. He helped him by casting the devil out of his son.

When people came to Jesus, they always received their deliverance! He provided them with whatever was needed—every time.

This same Jesus we see in the Bible ministering healing to the sick, deliverance to the oppressed and freedom for the captives, is the same Jesus who heals you today. So come to Him, trusting His mercy and compassion. Don't let previous prayer disappointments or past experiences keep you from the healing Jesus bought and paid for you to have. Even if you're struggling with doubt, reach out to Him anyway with a simple plea: "Lord, I believe; help my unbelief." Then get into God's Word and begin to meditate on healing scriptures that will build your faith to receive!

EXAMPLES OF JESUS HEALING PEOPLE:

THE WOMAN WITH AN INFIRMITY FOR EIGHTEEN YEARS

"Woman, you are loosed from your infirmity."

Now He was teaching in one of the synagogues on the Sabbath. And behold, there was a woman who had a spirit of infirmity eighteen years, and was bent over and could in no way raise herself up. But when Jesus saw her, He called her to Him and said to her, "Woman, you are loosed from your infirmity." And He laid His hands on her, and immediately she was made straight, and glorified God. But the ruler of the synagogue answered with indignation, because Jesus had healed on the Sabbath; and he said to the crowd, "There are six days on which men ought to work; therefore come and be healed on them, and not on the Sabbath day." The Lord then answered him and said, "Hypocrite! Does not each one of you on the Sabbath loose his ox or donkey from the stall, and lead it away to water it? So ought not this woman, being a daughter of Abraham, whom Satan has bound—[think of

> it!]—for eighteen years, be loosed from this bond on the Sabbath?" And when He said these things, all His adversaries were put to shame; and all the multitude rejoiced for all the glorious things that were done by Him (Luke 13:10-17).

A big part of receiving healing from Jesus is overcoming the lies of the devil. We've already dealt with some of those lies. We've seen that Jesus is always willing to heal us, that our sins cannot keep us from being healed, and that even if other people have prayed for us with no results, Jesus still stands ready to heal us.

But what if, like this woman, you have been sick for a long time?

In that case, the devil may have come to you with the lie that because you have suffered with this illness for so long, there's no hope for you. He may be telling you that the abnormal condition in your body is permanent. You can't be healed.

God, however, wants you to know that's not true. So much so, He made sure that this healing account in Luke 13 made it into the Bible just for you. He made sure to tell you that the bent-over woman Jesus met in the synagogue had been like that for eighteen years.

Eighteen years! Think about what it must have been like for that woman, being bent over for that long. She probably couldn't even remember how it felt to stand upright. Having spent so many years in that twisted condition, she probably envisioned herself that way for the rest of her life.

Jesus, however, did not.

The moment He saw her, He called for her and said, "Woman, you are loosed from your infirmity" (verse 12). The *English Standard Version* says, "Woman, you are freed from your disability." Then He laid His hands on her and "immediately she was made straight, and glorified God" (verse 13).

You'd think everyone in the synagogue would have been happy for her at that moment, but the ruler of the synagogue was upset. He thought Jesus was wrong for healing on the Sabbath. You have to watch out for people like that. Beware of naysayers in your life who say now is not the time for you to be healed. That's not what Jesus says!

Never do we see Jesus refusing to heal someone or telling them to come back again some other day. He always ministered healing right away to the sick who reached out to Him, even when others complained about it.

In fact, He strongly rebuked the rulers of the synagogue that day for saying He should have left that woman bound by that infirmity. "You frauds!" He said. "Each Sabbath every one of you regularly unties your cow or donkey from its stall, leads it out for water, and thinks nothing of it. So why isn't it all right for me to untie this daughter of Abraham and lead her from the stall where Satan has had her tied these eighteen years?" *(The Message,* verse 15).

Jesus wasn't like the religious rulers and experts of His day. They only cared about their rules and laws. He cared about people!

He cared about this woman so much, He didn't even wait for her to call on Him for help. He made the first move. He saw her and called out to her. He made it clear that Satan was responsible for her long-term illness, had compassion on her, and set her free.

Jesus desires to do the same for you. He sees you today just like He saw that woman. He cares about you, and He wants you healed of whatever is wrong with you. You are His. You belong to Him, and He wants you well.

Even if you have never been born again, Jesus sees you and wants you loosed from any infirmity. If you will believe and say, "Yes, I ought to be loosed, and I believe Jesus is the One to do it," His healing Anointing will come into you and make you well. It doesn't matter how far gone you are or how bound up you are. That's all it takes. Whatever you say, Jesus will do!

EXAMPLES OF JESUS HEALING PEOPLE:

THE TEN LEPERS

"Jesus, Master, have mercy on us!"

Now it happened as He went to Jerusalem that He passed through the midst of Samaria and Galilee. Then as He entered a certain village, there met Him ten men who were lepers, who stood afar off. And they lifted up their voices and said, "Jesus, Master, have mercy on us!" So when He saw them, He said to them, "Go, show yourselves to the priests." And so it was that as they went, they were cleansed. And one of them, when he saw that he was healed, returned, and with a loud voice glorified God, and fell down on his face at His feet, giving Him thanks. And he was a Samaritan. So Jesus answered and said, "Were there not ten cleansed? But where are the nine? Were there not any found who returned to give glory to God except this foreigner?" And He said to him, "Arise, go your way. Your faith has made you well" (Luke 17:11-19).

Although Jesus always ministered healing to everyone who came to Him to receive it, these verses remind us that not all healings manifest instantaneously.

Sometimes healing shows up in our body *after* we come to Jesus as we go on our way, believing we have received. Sometimes the symptoms of sickness disappear after we take Jesus at His Word and, without having felt anything or had any kind of dramatic experience, we act on it, simply believing that what He said is true.

Sometimes I've heard Christians say things like, "If only I could feel Jesus' touch on my fevered brow, I know I could be healed." But we don't need Jesus to appear and physically touch us to receive healing. The ten lepers didn't touch Him. They didn't get near Him at all.

They weren't like the bent-over woman in the synagogue who was so close to Jesus that He could lay His hand on her. They stood far away from Him. The *Amplified Bible, Classic Edition* says they "stood at a distance" (Luke 17:12).

Why were they standing far away?

Maybe because, as we've already discussed, lepers were social outcasts. They were considered unclean and unfit to come into contact with anyone other than their fellow lepers. That's probably why these ten men didn't approach Jesus directly. The Scripture doesn't say that they couldn't get near Him because of the crowd, as it does in other instances. So apparently, they could have come near Him but they felt unworthy.

Don't ever let the feeling that you are not good enough

or worthy enough keep you from coming to Jesus. Those kinds of feelings are of the devil. He delights in rehearsing all the reasons why you don't qualify to come boldly to Jesus and receive healing. But the devil is a liar and the father of lies (see John 8:44). The truth is that Jesus Himself has already qualified you. Through His death, burial and resurrection, He opened the way for you to come to Him anytime and "obtain mercy, and find grace to help in time of need" (Hebrews 4:16).

Healing is a manifestation of God's mercy!

The ten lepers cried out to Jesus saying, "Master, have *mercy* on us," and Jesus did exactly what they said. He had mercy on them by telling them how to receive their healing. "Go, show yourselves to the priests," He told them.

What happened as they acted on His Word?

Luke 17:14 says, "As they went, they were cleansed."

I'm so glad that verse is in the Bible. It assures us that we don't have to have some instantaneous manifestation to know we're healed. Although such things can happen, that's not where our focus is. We're looking to the Word, which says that by Jesus' stripes we *were* healed (1 Peter 2:24). So once we've believed and taken our stand on the Word, we can go our way, expecting to be healed as we go.

We can also learn from the example of the one leper who returned to Jesus after his healing manifested. "With a loud voice [he] glorified God, and fell down on his face at His feet, giving Him thanks" (Luke 17:15-16). This expression of gratitude opened the door for him to receive even more from Jesus. It gave Jesus the opportunity to say to him, "Thy faith hath made thee whole" (verse 19, *King James Version).*

It's one thing to be healed from the disease of leprosy. It's another to be made whole. That's restoration!

See how easy it is to receive from Jesus? He's so wonderful, gracious and kind that He did for all ten of those lepers exactly what they asked. He had mercy on them and healed them, and even did something extra for the one who returned to give thanks!

EXAMPLES OF JESUS HEALING PEOPLE:

THE CENTURION'S SERVANT

"Say the word, and my servant will be healed."

Now when He concluded all His sayings in the hearing of the people, He entered Capernaum. And a certain centurion's servant, who was dear to him, was sick and ready to die. So when he heard about Jesus, he sent elders of the Jews to Him, pleading with Him to come and heal his servant. And when they came to Jesus, they begged Him earnestly, saying that the one for whom He should do this was deserving, "for he loves our nation, and has built us a synagogue." Then Jesus went with them. And when He was already not far from the house, the centurion sent friends to Him, saying to Him, "Lord, do not trouble Yourself, for I am not worthy that You should enter under my roof. Therefore I did not even think myself worthy to come to You. But say the word, and my servant will be healed. For I also am a man placed under authority, having soldiers under me. And I say to one, 'Go,' and he goes; and to another, 'Come,' and he comes; and to my servant, 'Do this,' and he does it." When Jesus heard these things, He marveled at him, and turned around and said to the crowd that followed Him, "I say to you, I have not found such great faith, not even in Israel!" And those who were sent, returning to the house, found the servant well who had been sick (Luke 7:1-10).

In the account of the ten lepers, we saw they stood far off from Jesus because they considered themselves unworthy to come to Him. In this account of the centurion's servant, we initially see the opposite happen.

We see the centurion's representatives claiming that he actually was worthy to have Jesus come to his house. Mentioning all the wonderful things the centurion had done, they called him deserving. "He loves our nation, and has built us a synagogue," they said.

Jesus didn't say anything to them in response. He had not asked the centurion's representatives about his accomplishments or his good deeds. He never asked about such things because it had nothing to do with His willingness to heal.

Some people haven't understood this. They think they are worthy of healing due to their good works, but that's not supported in Scripture. Nowhere did Jesus instruct the disciples to go heal people who did good works. Nowhere did He say, "Find out who has been going to church, paying their tithes, and being a good person, and then I'll minister healing to them." No, in His instructions to His disciples, Jesus said, "Heal the sick, cleanse the lepers, raise the dead, cast out demons. Freely you have received, freely give" (Matthew 10:8).

Certainly, going to church is wonderful; so is bringing your tithes and offerings and serving others. But those things do not qualify you to be healed. Healing isn't something you earn. Healing belongs to you. It was purchased for you by the death, burial and resurrection of Jesus; and any sick person who will put their faith in Him qualifies to receive it.

In this account about the centurion, although Jesus didn't respond to his representatives boasting about the man's accomplishments, He still did what they said. He went with them to minister to the centurion's servant. But He didn't go because the centurion was good, He went because He Himself is good!

Before Jesus arrived at the man's house, however, the centurion sent Jesus another message. This one made it clear that, unlike his misguided representatives, the centurion did not expect Jesus to do what he asked because he was deserving. "Lord," he said, "I did not even think myself worthy to come to You. But say the word, and my servant will be healed."

The centurion said how he wanted it, and Jesus did it. According to the centurion's faith, it was done unto him.

He received from Jesus what he expected, and his servant was healed that same hour.

All Jesus asks of us is that we believe the Word of God. If we believe what He says, then we can expect to receive from Him.

EXAMPLES OF JESUS HEALING PEOPLE:

JAIRUS AND HIS DAUGHTER

"Come and lay Your hands on her, that she may be healed."

Now when Jesus had crossed over again by boat to the other side, a great multitude gathered to Him; and He was by the sea. And behold, one of the rulers of the synagogue came, Jairus by name. And when he saw Him, he fell at His feet and begged Him earnestly, saying, "My little daughter lies at the point of death. Come and lay Your hands on her, that she may be healed, and she will live." So Jesus went with him, and a great multitude followed Him and thronged Him.... While He was still speaking, some came from the ruler of the synagogue's house who said, "Your daughter is dead. Why trouble the Teacher any further?" As soon as Jesus heard the word that was spoken, He said to the ruler of the synagogue, "Do not be afraid; only believe." And He permitted no one to follow Him except Peter, James, and John the brother of James. Then He came to the house of the ruler of the synagogue, and saw a tumult and those who wept and wailed loudly. When He came

> in, He said to them, "Why make this commotion and weep? The child is not dead, but sleeping." And they ridiculed Him. But when He had put them all outside, He took the father and the mother of the child, and those who were with Him, and entered where the child was lying. Then He took the child by the hand, and said to her, "Talitha, cumi," which is translated, "Little girl, I say to you, arise." Immediately the girl arose and walked, for she was twelve years of age. And they were overcome with great amazement. But He commanded them strictly that no one should know it, and said that something should be given her to eat (Mark 5:21-24, 35-43).

Many of the religious leaders described in the Gospels, approached Jesus like they were experts. But in these verses, we see in Jairus, a ruler of the synagogue, a very different attitude. He came to Jesus in humility, believing to receive from Him what he needed.

He came in desperation and literally fell at Jesus' feet, begging Him to come to his house and heal his daughter.

The Bible doesn't tell us what Jairus' attitude toward Jesus had been before his daughter had gotten sick. But he might have been like some people today. They'll say they don't believe in healing or miracles…until they actually need one. Then they change their minds.

There is often a great softening that occurs in a person's

heart when they need a miracle. With no one else to turn to, those who once criticized Jesus will often turn to Him. How does He respond when they do? If they come to Him in faith, He responds to them just as He did to Jairus.

Jesus is so gracious and wonderful! When Jairus asked Him to come to his house and lay His hands on his daughter, Jesus did exactly what he said. He didn't tell Jairus that plan didn't suit Him. He didn't say to him, "No, I believe I'll handle this situation My way," or "I'd rather you bring your daughter here to Me." He just started walking with Jairus toward his house.

While they were on their way there, however, Jairus got news no parent ever wants to hear: He got word that his daughter was already dead. A bad report like that can spark fear in a person.

If you've received a negative report from a doctor, you may have felt that kind fear yourself. The dire diagnosis you've been given may be pressuring you to let go of your confidence in God's Word. But don't allow a negative report to convince you to abandon your faith that Jesus will heal you. Instead, follow the instructions Jesus gave in this situation.

He said to Jairus, "Do not be afraid; only believe" (verse 36). The *Amplified Bible, Classic Edition* says, "Do not be seized with alarm and struck with fear; only keep on believing."

Jesus said something else very interesting after hearing the bad report about Jairus' daughter. He said the only disciples who could go with Him to Jairus's house were Peter, James and John.

It's important who you surround yourself with when standing in faith. When you are believing the Word of God for healing, you need to look around at your circle of close friends. Are they standing with you? Or are they agreeing with the negative report?

Jesus apparently trusted Peter, James and John to agree with Him in that situation. So, He took them with Him into the room where Jairus's daughter was lying. Of all Jesus' disciples, Peter, James and John were the only ones who got to see Jesus take that little girl by the hand, tell her to arise, and give her back to her parents, alive and well.

We've seen this happen again and again when people came to Jesus for healing. Jairus said to Him, "Come and lay Your hand on her and she will live." Jesus came and touched her, and life came into her body. The centurion said, "Speak the word only and my servant will be healed." Jesus spoke the word, and his servant was healed.

Whatever someone said, Jesus did.

EXAMPLES OF JESUS HEALING PEOPLE:

THE WOMAN WITH THE ISSUE OF BLOOD

"If only I may touch His clothes, I shall be made well."

Now a certain woman had a flow of blood for twelve years, and had suffered many things from many physicians. She had spent all that she had and was no better, but rather grew worse. When she heard about Jesus, she came behind Him in the crowd and touched His garment. For she said, "If only I may touch His clothes, I shall be made well." Immediately the fountain of her blood was dried up, and she felt in her body that she was healed of the affliction. And Jesus, immediately knowing in Himself that power had gone out of Him, turned around in the crowd and said, "Who touched My clothes?" But His disciples said to Him, "You see the multitude thronging You, and You say, 'Who touched Me?'" And He looked around to see her who had done this thing. But the woman, fearing and trembling, knowing what had happened to her, came and fell down before Him and told Him the whole truth. And He said to her, "Daughter, your faith has made you well. Go in peace, and be healed of your affliction" (Mark 5:25-34).

If you've been battling a chronic illness for a long time, you may have had many of the same experiences this woman had. You may know what it's like to go to many doctors and spend a lot of money on doctors' bills. You may have been repeatedly in the hospital and rather than getting better, maybe, just like this woman, you actually got worse.

You may even think that since the doctors couldn't fix you, Jesus can't either. But nothing could be further from the truth.

When medical science doesn't know what to do, Jesus always does.

The woman in Mark 5 had heard enough about Jesus to believe this. The scriptures don't tell us exactly what she had heard, but someone had probably told her that He was going about doing good and healing all who were oppressed by the devil, for God was with Him (see Acts 10:38). Maybe she heard that whatever people were asking, Jesus was doing.

She obviously knew that anyone who got close enough to touch Him could be healed, "For she kept saying, If I only touch His garments, I shall be restored to health" (verse 28, *Amplified Bible, Classic Edition).*

What's more, she acted on what she said!

Given her condition, that took some determination. As the *New Living Translation* says, she "had suffered for twelve years with constant bleeding" (verse 25). I don't know all the problems she must have had with that kind of continual blood loss, but I'm sure she was fatigued, or even anemic. Her energy level must have been extremely low. So for her to press into the crowd and touch Jesus took a lot of effort on her part. But she did it anyway.

Why? Because she was tired of putting up with the illness. For years, it had been eating away at her life.

That's what chronic illness does. It eats away at your finances. It eats away at your time and energy, and it takes you away from other priorities. It keeps you from doing what you'd like to do for your family or at church. It prevents you from being the blessing you'd like to be to others, and keeps you from fully enjoying life.

Jesus doesn't want you to have to continue in that condition, although there is no shame or condemnation in it. He has a better solution for you than living with a longtime illness that restricts what you are able to do. He wants you to be free to love and serve others.

That's why God had this woman's story recorded in the Bible. He wants you to be healed just as she was.

How exactly was she healed?

Just the way she said she would be. She did not say, "If He lays hands on me, I will be healed." She didn't send messengers to Him, or ask Him to come to her house, or cry out to Him as people did in some of the other accounts of healing in the Gospels. She said, "If I may but touch His garment, I will be made whole," and she got exactly what she said. When she came behind Jesus in the crowd and touched His clothes, it was done to her according to her faith. Power flowed out of Jesus into her body, and she was healed of that plague.

"But Gloria," you might say, "I can't physically touch Jesus like she did."

You don't need to physically touch Him. After Jesus was raised from the dead, because He sent the Holy Spirit to the earth to continue His ministry, now the power of God is present to heal all the time! Even when you wake up in the middle of the night, the power of God is present to heal you right where you are because God is there.

Your faith causes His power to come into your body. Today, just as in the days when the Bible was written, it is according to your faith that it is done unto you (Matthew 9:29). And just as in the case of this woman in Mark 5, your faith is expressed through your words.

If you've had problems getting healed, you might want to check up on what you've been saying. You might want to see if you're speaking in agreement with the Bible.

Isaiah 53:5 says, for example, "By His stripes we are healed," so if you've been saying, "I am sick," you're not agreeing with what the Word says. Someone could have even prayed for you, but if you are talking sickness and disease, you're working against yourself. It's when you speak the Word that deliverance comes.

Mark 11:23-24 confirms this. There, Jesus said, "Whoever says to this mountain, 'Be removed and be cast into the sea,' and does not doubt in his heart, but believes that those things he says will be done, he will have whatever he says. Therefore I say to you, whatever things you ask when you pray, believe that you receive them, and you will have them."

Your words might not come to pass immediately; you might not see the change in your body the instant you start saying you're healed. But if you continue saying what the Bible says about you, healing *will* come.

Kenneth E. Hagin, founder of Kenneth Hagin Ministries in Tulsa, Oklahoma, compared the healing power of God to electricity. With electricity, you can have an outlet, but until you plug something into it, like your TV or your toaster, nothing is going to happen even though the power is there. That's how it is with the power of God. It is present to heal. But to experience it, we must plug in our faith by expecting and acting on it.

The woman who had the issue of blood got healed because she plugged into the power of God. When she pressed through the crowd to get to Jesus, her faith caused the healing Anointing that was on Him to go into her body. He didn't even know she was there until

He felt that power flow out of Him, and by then it had already been done unto her according to her faith.

She had said, "If I may but touch His garment, I will be made whole," and that's exactly what happened. She touched Jesus' garment, and she was made whole.

EXAMPLES OF JESUS HEALING PEOPLE:

BLIND BARTIMAEUS

"Jesus, Son of David, have mercy on me!"

Now they came to Jericho. As He [Jesus] went out of Jericho with His disciples and a great multitude, blind Bartimaeus, the son of Timaeus, sat by the road begging. And when he heard that it was Jesus of Nazareth, he began to cry out and say, "Jesus, Son of David, have mercy on me!" Then many warned him to be quiet; but he cried out all the more, "Son of David, have mercy on me!" So Jesus stood still and commanded him to be called. Then they called the blind man, saying to him, "Be of good cheer. Rise, He is calling you." And throwing aside his garment, he rose and came to Jesus. So Jesus answered and said to him, "What do you want Me to do for you?" The blind man said to Him, "Rabboni, that I may receive my sight." Then Jesus said to him, "Go your way; your faith has made you well." And immediately he received his sight and followed Jesus on the road (Mark 10:46-52).

What always stands out to me when I read about the healing of Bartimaeus is this: He was persistent! He didn't let the circumstances, or the words of other people, deter him from receiving his healing.

He reminds me of a young boy whom Oral Roberts, a well-known healing evangelist of the twentieth century, used to talk about who came to one of his meetings. He was determined to be healed, but because of the crowd, the boy was not able to get to Brother Roberts to receive prayer. After the service, as Oral was leaving the auditorium, feeling completely exhausted after ministering one by one to so many people, he saw the little boy sitting at a table in one of the side rooms. Obviously crippled, the boy had his crutches propped up next to him.

Brother Roberts said, "Son, what are you doing here?"

"I am supposed to be healed today," the boy said.

Wearily, Brother Roberts explained the situation. "I don't think I have enough strength left to pray for one more person," he said.

"I don't know anything about that," the boy replied, "I just know that I am supposed to be healed today."

Hearing those words, Oral sensed the power of God come on him and said, "Son, when I lay my hands on you, you let your faith go."

He laid his hands on him, and that little boy let his faith go.

When I heard Brother Roberts share this story, the

boy had grown up and was now a man in his mid-forties. He was still healed.

All of us, as believers, ought to have the same attitude that little boy had where healing is concerned. He wasn't moved by the fact that Brother Roberts was tired. He knew that day he was supposed to be healed.

That's how Bartimaeus was. He had obviously heard of Jesus, and that everywhere He went, people were healed. He probably even knew Jesus had specifically said that He was anointed to proclaim "recovery of sight to the blind" (Luke 4:18). So when he found out Jesus was passing right by where he was sitting, he decided, *I am supposed to be healed today!* and began yelling, "Jesus, Son of David, have mercy on me!"

He didn't care that the people around him rebuked him and commanded him to shut up. He wasn't moved by their mean and belittling attitude toward him. We don't know exactly what they said, but it was probably something like *Bartimaeus, you blind old fool. Jesus is too busy to waste time on a beggar like you! Quit hollering at Him! Shut your mouth!*

Bartimaeus, however, didn't pay any attention to them. Instead, he cried out even louder!

What happened as a result? Jesus stopped in His tracks. Faith stopped Him. Faith will always get Jesus' attention. So, He stood still and commanded that Bartimaeus be brought to Him (Luke 18:40).

Suddenly, the people who had been telling Bartimaeus to shut up and giving him such a hard time changed their tune. They said to Bartimaeus, "Be of good cheer. Rise, He is calling you."

People can be so wishy-washy. Don't let other people tell you what to do. Don't let their negative comments, attitudes and ideas dissuade you from believing what the Word of God says. Be like Bartimaeus. He knew exactly what he was believing to receive. No matter what anyone else said, he had determined he was supposed to be healed that day. So he had his answer ready when, in response to his cry of faith, Jesus asked him, "What do you want Me to do for you?"

Think about that question for a moment. It was simple, because Jesus always made it simple for people to receive from Him.

If He stood before you right now and asked, "What do you want Me to do for you?" how would you respond? What would be your answer? You need to have it ready, because no matter what type of sickness or disease you may be facing, Jesus stands before you now, just like He stood before Bartimaeus, asking, "What do you want Me to do for you today? Just say it, and it is done."

You might say to me, "Gloria, how can you be so confident of this?"

Because Jesus is the same today as He was the day He healed Bartimaeus.

Think again about what the angel said to Jesus' disciples at His ascension: "This same Jesus, which is taken up from you into heaven, shall so come in like manner as ye have seen him go into heaven" (Acts 1:11, *King James Version).* If Jesus is going to be the same when He comes back as He was when He left, that means that between then and now, He is the same wonderful, gracious, healing Jesus.

This same Jesus is saying to you today, "What do you want Me do for you?"

Bartimaeus answered that question, "I want to see," and he received his sight. What Bartimaeus said, Jesus did.

This same Jesus will do the same for you!

CHAPTER 5

BE ENCOURAGED: NO SITUATION IS TOO HARD FOR JESUS

CHAPTER 5

BE ENCOURAGED: NO SITUATION IS TOO HARD FOR JESUS

You know by now that the devil will lie to you to keep you from receiving your healing. But I want to add another word of warning about a specific tactic he likes to use. When trying to undermine your faith, he likes to remind you of all your failures and past mistakes.

As Keith Moore, one of my favorite preachers, puts it, "The devil uses the pile-up principle." He tries to pile up all the ways you've missed it and all the reasons you shouldn't be healed so that you feel overwhelmed. "You are no good," he'll say. "You've screwed up your entire life. Your mother told you that you would never amount to anything, and she was right. You've made a lot of stupid choices, and now you're going to have to live with the results."

If you let him, the devil will pile up thoughts of rejection and failure until you can hardly hold your head up. So don't let him! When he starts talking to you like that, tell him to get out of your face. Quit listening to him and think instead about what Jesus told the paralytic man who got healed when his friends let him down through the roof.

Remember how Jesus dealt with the condemnation the devil had piled on that man? He said, "Which is easier, to say…'Your sins are forgiven you,' or to say, 'Arise, take up your bed and walk'? But that you may know that the Son of Man has power on earth to forgive sins…I say to you, arise, take up your bed, and go to your house" (Mark 2:9-11).

In other words, Jesus said that the same power that cleanses away sin also heals the physical body. It is the same Spirit, the same Anointing. So when you come to Him, you can receive total forgiveness and receive your healing at the same time!

Once when I was teaching about this at one of our meetings, there was a girl in the congregation who had been paralyzed on one side of her body for years. She wanted to be healed, but she was feeling condemned because she had stolen a book from our book table. When she heard me preach that she could be forgiven and healed at the same time, however, she was healed. What a wonderful display of the compassion and goodness of God!

Don't let anything stop you from receiving your healing from Jesus.

James 5:14-15 says, "Is anyone among you sick? Let

him call for the elders of the church, and let them pray over him, anointing him with oil in the name of the Lord. And the prayer of faith will save the sick, and the Lord will raise him up. And if he has committed sins, he will be forgiven."

"But Gloria," somebody might say, "you don't know how many awful sins I've committed!"

It doesn't matter. That's why the gospel of the kingdom of God is such good news. The devil could work on your life for many years, lying to you and convincing you to live in sin. He could tempt you to murder, steal, prostitute yourself and live in perversion, deceiving you into wasting years of your life. But in one moment of time, you can hear the gospel, and it can all be wiped away.

It's true. Simply hearing about the Lord Jesus Christ and what He has done for you can change everything. Once you realize He isn't holding anything against you and you turn to Him, in an instant, you become a new creation (2 Corinthians 5:17). It's as though you had never sinned at all.

God loves you! He takes pleasure in forgiving and making you new on the inside.

Some of the most powerful people being used by God today, were, at one time, murderers or drug addicts. I know one man who was on death row. He heard the Word of God through the ministry materials we send to inmates and gave his life to Jesus. Then he started believing God for his sentence to be commuted. As a result, he not only got off death row, but he got released from prison.

After he got out, he looked at our ministry schedule to find out where our meetings were, and he would go ahead of us into that city and get a job until we got there. Then, he would quit his job and come to the meetings to hear the Word of God. He traveled from one meeting of ours to another, and he is a great man of God today.

You might have thought you were called to ministry for years, and yet you've continued to live in a sinful lifestyle, thinking you could never get back in the will of God. But compassion is still reaching out to you. If you will receive His mercy and commit your life to Him, God can get you back on track. He can set you straight and help you get on the path that He preordained for you to walk from the time you were born.

It is never too late. No matter how far gone you are, or how big of a mess you may have made out of your life, you can partake of the free favors of God today.

If you need proof, read about the madman of Gadara. Few people today are as far gone as he was when Jesus ministered to him. He was not only demon-possessed, but for a long time, he had been homeless, running around naked, and living in the cemetery! Mark 5:4-7 says:

> He had often been bound with shackles and chains. And the chains had been pulled apart by him, and the shackles broken in pieces; neither could anyone tame him. And always, night and day, he was in the mountains and in the tombs, crying out and cutting himself with stones. When he saw Jesus from afar, he ran and worshiped Him. And he cried out with a loud voice and said, "What have I to do with You, Jesus, Son of the Most High God? I implore You by God that You do not torment me."

How did Jesus respond to this wild, demonized man? As graciously and compassionately as He responded to all the other people we've read about. He ordered the unclean spirit to come out of the man, set him free and left him "clothed and in his right mind" (verse 15).

If the madman of Gadara wasn't too much for Jesus to handle, neither are you! Your situation is not too far gone for Him to fix! You are not going to scare Him with your problems or addictions. He loves you. He is not moved by what you have done or your background. He has what it takes to make you right, make your mind sound, and deliver you from whatever has had you in bondage.

I have friends whose brains were ruined by drugs. When they started feeding on the Word of God, the physical damage to their brains was reversed, and they were restored. I also have friends who, in addition to having been addicted to drugs, were also violent to the point of being murderous. Yet they have been delivered by God and are some of the sweetest people you could ever meet. They have compassion for everyone, especially for those who are in the same condition they were. The compassion of Jesus comes through them to minister to people.

That's what happens when Jesus heals and delivers you—you are then able to minister to others (2 Corinthians 1:4). You actually make a way for them to be healed and set free.

There is nothing more powerful than the personal testimony of someone whose life has been changed by the power of God. It gives people hope. It speaks to them of God's power and lovingkindness. Think of all the lost people who live around you; they don't have a clue that God cares anything about them. They don't know that God heals. They don't know that He will put bread on their table and help them.

After Jesus restored the madman of Gadara to his right mind, He said to him, "'Go home to your friends, and tell them what great things the Lord has done for you, and how He has had compassion on you.' And he departed and began to proclaim in Decapolis all that Jesus had done for him; and all marveled" (Mark 5:19-20).

It's interesting to note that although people in that region had once rejected Jesus, when He returned there, the people received Him. Do you know why? Because of that man's testimony.

There is power in your testimony to change a household, a workplace, a town, a city or a region. So, let Jesus give you that testimony. He hasn't changed at all since the days when He walked this earth and "went about all the cities and villages, teaching in their synagogues, preaching the gospel of the kingdom, and healing *every* sickness and *every* disease among the people" (Matthew 9:35).

Jesus hasn't lost any of His power or His compassion.

He is the same yesterday, today and forever.

He is still the same Jesus!

CHAPTER 6

A PRAYER FOR HEALING

CHAPTER 6

A PRAYER FOR HEALING

What is it that *you* want from the Lord? Tell Him what it is. Name it and say, "I want to receive this from You today, Lord." Then pray the following prayer aloud from your heart:

> I confess Jesus Christ as Lord over my life—spirit, soul and body.
>
> I receive the power of God to save me, make me sound, whole, delivered and healed.
>
> I act on the Word of God, and I receive the power of God.
>
> Sickness, disease and pain: I resist you in the Name of Jesus. You are not the will of God for me. I will not tolerate sickness in my life. Leave my presence. I will never allow you back.
>
> My days of sickness and disease are over. Jesus says I am whole.
>
> The power of sickness has been forever broken over my life.

Sickness shall no longer lord it over me. Jesus is my Lord, my Deliverer, my Savior, my Healer.

Sin shall no longer lord it over me.

Fear shall no longer lord it over me.

I have been redeemed from the curse of the Law, and I proclaim freedom in Jesus' Name.

Today it is done unto me as I believe that Jesus Christ is the same yesterday, today and forever.

Today I receive, in Jesus' Name.

I take authority over every evil spirit, every sickness and disease.

I take authority over every situation in my body that needs to be repaired.

I take authority over every part of my body that is broken.

In the Name of the Lord Jesus Christ, I receive the healing Anointing of Jesus flowing into me from the top of my head to the soles of my feet.

Ears, be opened in Jesus' Name.

Eyes, be opened in Jesus' Name.

I rebuke every kind of blood disease.

I rebuke any kind of heart problems in the Name of Jesus. I command my heart to be whole. Arteries, you be clear and restored in Jesus' Name.

Kidneys, be healed.

Liver, be healed.

Cells in my body, be normal.

I speak to every cancer cell and command you to die in the Name of Jesus. I rebuke you out of my body.

I rebuke any kind of tumor or abnormal growth.

Body, be healed and repaired in the Name of the Lord Jesus Christ.

I speak to weakness and command it to be gone.

I command the Anointing of God to flow into me and strengthen my body.

My body is strengthened, in Jesus' Name.

I speak to my limbs. I speak to my spinal cord. Be made whole.

I speak to any kind of infirmity that would hold me back.

I speak to any kind of infirmity that would keep me from being mobile and walking.

I speak to any kind of infirmity that would keep me from being strong and healthy.

I have a strong mind.

I speak to *any* infirmity to leave my body now, in the Name of Jesus. I am free.

I walk. I run. I skip. I jump. In the Name of the Lord Jesus Christ, I am made whole.

I rebuke arthritis off my body.

I command it to let go of my body, to let go of my bones, to let go of me, in the Name of Jesus.

I rebuke pain out of my body. I command my back to be normal.

All the bones in my body are healed, repaired and normal, in the Name of the Lord Jesus Christ.

Every disease has to go from my body, in Jesus' Name.

Thank You, Lord, for my deliverance. Thank You for my healing.

I am healed. I am restored. I am made whole, in the Name of Jesus.

I am able to move, to walk, to run. I am free. I am strong.

God has made me strong. God is renewing my youth like the eagle's.

I am well. My mind is sound.

I rebuke every addiction. I will have no evil addiction in my body.

The power of drugs, alcohol, tobacco, pornography and perversion is gone from me in Jesus' Name.

I am free. Whom the Son sets free is free indeed.

Glory to God! Thank You, Jesus!

Prayer for Salvation and Baptism in the Holy Spirit

Heavenly Father, I come to You in the Name of Jesus. Your Word says, "Whosoever shall call on the name of the Lord shall be saved" (Acts 2:21). I am calling on You. I pray and ask Jesus to come into my heart and be Lord over my life according to Romans 10:9–10: "If thou shalt confess with thy mouth the Lord Jesus, and shalt believe in thine heart that God hath raised him from the dead, thou shalt be saved. For with the heart man believeth unto righteousness; and with the mouth confession is made unto salvation." I do that now. I confess that Jesus is Lord, and I believe in my heart that God raised Him from the dead. I repent of sin. I renounce it. I renounce the devil and everything he stands for. Jesus is my Lord.

I am now reborn! I am a Christian—a child of Almighty God! I am saved! You also said in Your Word, "If ye then, being evil, know how to give good gifts unto your children: HOW MUCH MORE shall your heavenly Father give the Holy Spirit to them that ask him?" (Luke 11:13). I'm also asking You to fill me with the Holy Spirit. Holy Spirit, rise up within me as I praise God. I fully expect to speak with other tongues as You give me the utterance (Acts 2:4). In Jesus' Name. Amen!

Begin to praise God for filling you with the Holy Spirit. Speak those words and syllables you receive—not in your own language, but the language given to you by the Holy Spirit. You have to use your own voice. God will not force you to speak. Don't be concerned with how it sounds. It is a heavenly language!

Continue with the blessing God has given you and pray in the spirit every day.

You are a born-again, Spirit-filled believer. You'll never be the same!

Find a good church that boldly preaches God's Word and obeys it. Become part of a church family who will love and care for you as you love and care for them.

We need to be connected to each other. It increases our strength in God. It's God's plan for us.

Make it a habit to watch the *Believer's Voice of Victory* broadcast and VICTORY Channel and become a doer of the Word, who is blessed in his doing (James 1:22-25).

About the Author

Gloria Copeland is a noted author and minister of the gospel whose teaching ministry is known throughout the world. Believers worldwide know her through Believers' Conventions, Victory Campaigns, magazine articles, teaching audios and videos, and the daily and Sunday *Believer's Voice of Victory* television broadcast, which she hosts with her husband, Kenneth Copeland. She is known for Healing School, which she began teaching and hosting in 1979 at KCM meetings. Gloria delivers the Word of God and the keys to victorious Christian living to millions of people every year.

Gloria is author of the New York Times best-seller, *God's Master Plan for Your Life* and *Live Long, Finish Strong,* as well as numerous other favorites, including *God's Will for You, Walk With God, God's Will Is Prosperity, Hidden Treasures* and *To Know Him.* She has also co-authored several books with her husband, including *Family Promises, Healing Promises* and the best-selling daily devotionals, *From Faith to Faith* and *Pursuit of His Presence.*

She holds an honorary doctorate from Oral Roberts University. In 1994, Gloria was voted Christian Woman of the Year, an honor conferred on women whose example demonstrates outstanding Christian leadership. Gloria is also the co-founder and vice president of Kenneth Copeland Ministries in Fort Worth, Texas.

Learn more about Kenneth Copeland Ministries
by visiting our website at **kcm.org**

Renew your mind to the truth that God wants you well! Develop your faith with these life-changing messages and healing testimonies from Gloria's Healing School throughout the years.

WATCH ON

VICTORY CHANNEL®

24/7 Faith Teaching

Find all the ways to watch!
govictory.com/channelfinder

Download the Go VICTORY app!
iOS

Believer's Voice of

VICTORY™

When The LORD first spoke to Kenneth and Gloria Copeland about starting the *Believer's Voice of Victory* magazine...

He said: *This is your seed. Give it to everyone who ever responds to your ministry, and don't ever allow anyone to pay for a subscription!*

For more than 50 years, it has been the joy of Kenneth Copeland Ministries to bring the good news to believers. Readers enjoy teaching from ministers who write from lives of living contact with God, and testimonies from believers experiencing victory through God's Word in their everyday lives.

Today, the *BVOV* magazine is mailed monthly, bringing encouragement and blessing to believers around the world. Many even use it as a ministry tool, passing it on to others who desire to know Jesus and grow in their faith!

Request your FREE subscription to the *Believer's Voice of Victory* magazine today!

Go to **freevictory.com** to subscribe online, or call us at **1-800-600-7395** (U.S. only) or **+1-817-852-6000.**

We're Here for You!®

Your growth in God's Word and your victory in Jesus are at the very center of our hearts. In every way God has equipped us, we will help you deal with the issues facing you, so you can be the **victorious overcomer** He has planned for you to be.

The mission of Kenneth Copeland Ministries is about all of us growing and going together. Our prayer is that you will take full advantage of all the Lord has given us to share with you.

Wherever you are in the world, you can watch the *Believer's Voice of Victory* broadcast on television (check your local listings), kcm.org and digital streaming devices like Roku. You can also watch the broadcast as well as programs from dozens of ministers you can trust on our 24/7 faith network—Victory Channel. Visit govictory.com for show listings and all the ways to watch.

Our website, **kcm.org,** gives you access to every resource we've developed for your victory. And, you can find contact information for our international offices in Africa, Australia, Canada, Europe, Ukraine, Latin America and our headquarters in the United States.

Each office is staffed with devoted men and women, ready to serve and pray with you. You can contact the worldwide office nearest you for assistance, and you can call us for prayer at our U.S. number, +1-817-852-6000, every day of the week!

We encourage you to connect with us often and let us be part of your everyday walk of faith!

Jesus Is LORD!

Kenneth & Gloria Copeland

Kenneth and Gloria Copeland